Note to Parents

This book can't make the rain go away—but it *can* help you turn a rainy day into a day full of fun—and learning—for your child.

For quiet times, your preschooler will enjoy listening to the stories and poems. For livelier moments, there are puzzles and activity pages, plus lots of ideas for indoor play.

With preschoolers, playing is learning. Reading to your child is the best way to prepare your child for learning to read in school. And while your child is having fun with favorite Disney friends and enjoying the many activities in *It's Raining, It's Pouring,* he or she is developing important skills designed to build readiness for school: eye-hand coordination and following directions (pages 12-13), visual perception (16-17), days of week and numbers 1-7 (18-31), word meanings (32-33), following directions (38-39), and whole-body coordination (42-43). And your child will find out some interesting things about clouds and rainbows (36-38) and things that float (40-41), as well.

Make-and-do ideas that require some preparation are in a special section that begins on page 39. Most of the things you'll need can be found in the home. The Jiminy Cricket symbol appears wherever your help may be needed.

Is it raining? Even if it isn't, open this book and share the fun. It will make your preschooler's day a bit brighter—and perhaps yours, too.

It's Raining,
It's Pouring!

Bad-Weather Fundays

Published by
World Book Encyclopedia, Inc.
a Scott Fetzer company
Chicago

The Log Ride

The Seven Dwarfs had just finished work. As they set out for home, the sky began to darken. Lightning flashed, and thunder roared.

"It's going to start pouring," said Doc. "Let's head for cover." So the Dwarfs ran to a nearby cave.

Just as the Dwarfs got inside, the rain began to pour.
Loud claps of thunder shook the mountain. But the noise
didn't disturb Sleepy. He was already asleep.

"It's just like him to fall asleep," grumbled Grumpy.

"Don't worry," said Happy. "The rain will stop soon."

But the rain didn't stop. Doc knew that Snow White would be worried about them. It was raining harder than ever. The path down the mountain had turned to mud.

"We can't stay here any longer," said Doc. "Sleepy, wake up! We have to get going!"

6

So the Seven Dwarfs lined up—first Doc, then Grumpy,
Happy, Sleepy, Sneezy, Bashful, and Dopey.

Off they went, slip-slopping down the mountain. Dopey got stuck in
the mud, and Doc and Grumpy pulled him out.

"Dopey, watch where you're going," grumped Grumpy. He barely
had the words out of his mouth when he got stuck, too.

When the Dwarfs got to the bottom of the mountain, they saw that the path through the forest was flooded.

"We'll never get home," Bashful said sadly.

"I have an idea," said Doc. "Let's ride home." And he pointed to a log lying in the water.

"That will never work," said Grumpy. "Even if the log will float, how will we get it to move?"

"We'll use tree branches for oars," said Doc.

"Looks like fun," said Happy. "Hop on, everybody!"
So the Dwarfs climbed on. "Forward, row!" shouted Doc.
And off they went.

"What's that noise?" asked Grumpy. "It sounds like a wild animal about to attack us."

"Don't worry," said Sneezy. "It's only —ah—ah—ah—Sleepy snoring. Ah—choo!"

Before long the Dwarfs spotted their little house. Snow White ran out to greet them. "Oh, thank goodness you're all safe," she said. "I was so worried!"

"Of course we're safe," said Doc. "We just got a little wet —and that didn't hurt anybody. Besides, we didn't have to walk home. We got a ride!"

A Walk in the Rain

Happy and Bashful are taking a walk in the rain. You can go with them. Follow the path with your finger.

Happy and Bashful walked out the front door of the Seven Dwarfs' house.

1 First they walked to the wishing well. (When you get there, make a wish.)

4 Happy and Bashful followed the stepping stones home. Make your fingers step across. If you hurry, you might beat the Dwarfs home.

2 Then Happy and Bashful walked to the hollow tree. They looked inside. What do you see there?

3 Next Happy and Bashful hopped across the bridge. You hop across, too.

Rain, Rain

It's Raining

It's raining, it's pouring,
The old man is snoring;
He went to bed
And bumped his head
And couldn't get up the morning.

Mother Goose

Rain

Rain on the green grass,
Rain on the tree,
Rain on the housetop,
But not on me.

Mother Goose

Rain

The rain is raining all around,
   It falls on field and tree,
It rains on the umbrellas here,
   And on the ships at sea.

      Robert Louis Stevenson

To the Rain

Rain, rain, go away.
Come again another day,
Little Bashful wants to play.

Rain, rain, go to Spain,
Never show your face again.

      Mother Goose

Help the Seven Dwarfs

"It's raining, it's pouring!" Grumpy cried. All of the Seven Dwarfs ran inside—and they left some of their favorite things out in the yard.

Can you find what the Dwarfs left behind? Look for these things:

Doc's dish   Sneezy's snake   Sleepy's slipper

Grumpy's grapes   Bashful's ball

Happy's hat   Dopey's daisies

The Seven Dwarfs and the Bigger House

One Monday morning when the Seven Dwarfs woke up, it was pouring down rain. The Dwarfs couldn't go outside, so they sat around all day, listening to the rain. Grumpy grumbled. Sneezy sneezed. Sleepy snored.

Finally Happy started popping corn over the fire. "Too much noise!" grumped Grumpy. "Sneezy sneezing! Sleepy snoring! Happy popping corn! This place is too small for us. We need a bigger house."

Tuesday it rained even harder. Right after lunch, the Dwarfs heard a soft tap-tap at the door. Doc opened it and saw a mother deer and her fawn. They were dripping wet and shivering.

"Goodness," said Doc. "Come on in and get dry."

On Wednesday, the Dwarfs heard a loud THUMP at the door. Doc opened it. "Oh, my!" he said. In walked a brown bear and her two cubs. They were dripping wet, and the cubs looked very sad.

That evening, two clip-clopping deer and three snoring bears joined the Seven Dwarfs by the fire. Even Happy was beginning to think the house was too small.

On Thursday, Happy spotted four
wet squirrels clinging to a tree branch.
"Come on in, little ones," he called.
After all, four little squirrels wouldn't
take up much more room.

But with two clip-clopping deer,
three snoring bears, four chattering
squirrels, and Seven Dwarfs sitting by
the fire, the house seemed very small,
indeed.

On Friday, the Dwarfs heard something fluttering at the window. Bashful opened it. The rain blew in, and five of Snow White's doves blew in, too. They fluttered their wet feathers—all over Grumpy.

Now there were two clip-clopping deer, three snoring bears, four chattering squirrels, five fluttering doves, and the Seven Dwarfs crowded all around the fireplace. The house seemed smaller than ever!

By Saturday, everyone was tired of the rain. That night, Sneezy heard a tiny scratching at the door. "I'll see who's there," he said. Six shivering little rabbits were huddled on the doorstep.

"Ah—ah—ah—hop right in! Ah—choo!" Sneezy said.
"Come and get warm by our fire."

"Too crowded in here," Grumpy
grumbled. "No room for us folks. I'm
going to bed!" And all the Dwarfs
followed him, because Grumpy was
right.

With two clip-clopping deer, three snoring bears, four chattering squirrels, five fluttering doves, and six hopping rabbits, there was no room for the Seven Dwarfs to sit by the fire.

When the Dwarfs woke up on Sunday, the sky was blue. The Seven Dwarfs and all the animals stepped out into the warm sunlight. Slowly, the animals moved off into the forest. Then the Dwarfs went back inside the house.

"Why, look how big the house is!" Grumpy said. "It didn't look this big before."

"I know why," Happy chuckled. "With so many visitors stuffed inside, I'll bet the house got bigger."

And everyone agreed that it really must have happened that way!

Fun with Up and Down

The Seven Dwarfs are happy that the rain has
finally stopped. But now they have a lot of work
to do. The Dwarfs have to fix the roof and
shutters and clean up the yard.

   Look at the picture. Find everyone who
is *up*. Find everyone who is *down*.

up in
the air

down on
the ground

down on the ground

up on the chimney

up in the tree

up on the roof

up on a ladder

up in the tree

down on the ground

33

Clouds and Rainbows

"Doc, where does rain come from?" asked Sleepy.
"Rain comes from rain clouds," said Doc.
"Oh," said Sleepy. "But which clouds are rain clouds?"

Doc took Sleepy outside and showed him a rain cloud.
Do you see the cloud Doc is pointing at?

"How can I find a rainbow?" asked Sleepy.

"Look for one when the sun comes out while it's raining," said Doc. "Stand with the sun behind you and the rain in front of you. I'll bet you'll see one then."

Sleepy did that—and he saw a big, beautiful rainbow. Do you see it, too? What colors do you see?

Things You Can Do

A rainy day is a good time to make things. Here are the Seven Dwarfs' favorite make-it-yourself ideas for you to try.

Happy Says

Happy likes to make up rainy-day games to play, and all of the Dwarfs like to play them. One of their favorite games is "Happy says."

You can play "Happy says," too. Here's how.

"Watch and listen and do what I do—but only if I tell you to," says Happy. "If I say *Happy says,* then do what I do. If I *don't* say *Happy says,* stand still. Listen carefully, because I'm going to try to fool you. Are you ready?"

"Happy says, *Point to your toe.* (You should do that, because I said *Happy says.*)"

"Happy says, *Squat down*. (You should do that, too. I said *Happy says*.)"

"*Touch your toes with your hands*. Did I fool you? You shouldn't touch your toes, because I didn't say *Happy says*. If you made a mistake, you take my place and try to fool someone."

Tub and Puddle Fun

Every time it rained, there was a big puddle on the path in front of the Seven Dwarfs' house. Grumpy liked to splash in it. Dopey liked to look at himself in it. And all the Dwarfs liked to float things in it.

Here are some of the things the Seven Dwarfs did. You can try them, too—and you don't need to wait until it rains. The bathtub, a dishpan, or the sink will work just fine.

Some things float and some things don't. Find some of these things. See which ones will float.

toothpick   penny   teaspoon   stone   wooden spoon

cork   pencil   plastic bowl leaf   marble

Get a small jar with a lid. Screw the lid on tight. See if the jar floats.

Take off the lid. Let the jar fill with water. Does the jar float now?

Make a tiny boat. Save half an eggshell. Chew some gum and stick a small piece inside.

Use a toothpick and paper to make a sail. Stick the toothpick into the gum. Sail your tiny boat across the sink or tub.

Inside-Outside Games

The rain had almost stopped, and the sun was trying to shine. "I know what I'll do," Happy thought. "I'll make a game we can play inside—and take outside when the rain is over."

Here are two inside-outside games you can make.

Find three cardboard tubes from bathroom tissue. Paste or tape a funny picture on each one. Then arrange the tubes likc this.

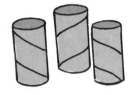

Get a small ball. Play "Bowl 'Em Over." Roll the ball at the tubes. Try to knock down all three tubes at once.

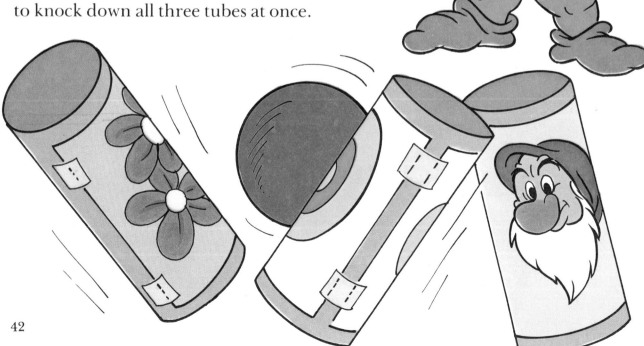

Use old socks to make beanbags.
Cut off the tops. Fill each sock foot
with dried beans and sew it shut.
Use small stitches so the beans won't
fall out.

Make a game for your beanbags.
Paint a big lion face on a box. Then
cut out the mouth. Play "Feed the
Lion" with your friends. Try to
throw beanbags in the lion's mouth.

Jiminy Cricket says,
"Your child may need
help with sewing and
cutting."